Rhythms i
and the cc

Rudolf Meyer

Rhythms
in human beings
and the cosmos

Floris Books

Translated by Donald Maclean

First published in German under the title
*Rhythmische Geheimnisse im Menschenwesen
und im Kosmos*
by Verlag Urachhaus, Stuttgart, 1956
First published in English in 1985 by Floris Books

British Library Cataloguing in Publication Data

Meyer, Rudolf
Rhythms in human beings and the cosmos.
1. Man—Influence of environment
I. Title   II. Rhythmische Geheimnisse im
Menschenwesen und im Kosmos. *English*
133   BF774

ISBN 0-86315-019-5

Printed in Great Britain
at the University Press, Oxford

Contents

1. The rhythm of waking and sleeping

The catastrophes which have overtaken the world have their origins primarily in unsolved social problems. All attempts at political reorganization of the world, all purely economic measures, however boldly planned, have proved inadequate. For there is no system which can guarantee a truly social order unless the individuals growing up into it can become social beings; that is beings who have understanding for each other and who can therefore bear with one another. Hitherto mankind has lived from a heritage of social forces. The powers of blood and tradition, the unifying forces of nationality and of religious customs were what maintained a more or less healthy living and working together. These are all dying away. Any new impetus for social living, therefore, can only be found at the present point of human evolution through a *knowledge* which can see into the action of social and antisocial forces of human nature.

A simple fact may serve as a starting point in our search for the social motivating forces. We can observe in ourselves how at certain times we can be receptive towards our fellow human beings, while at other times we are irritated by their weaknesses and less sensitive to their being. Often there is a very simple reason for this behaviour: we are overtired. But as soon as we are able to get enough sleep we become more human, tolerant and sympathetic. The rhythmical swing between waking and sleeping enables us to live as social beings. When we are awake, through our senses we are open to the world around us; we develop an interest for what others are doing and so we naturally take our place in a social order. In sleep, following an irresistible urge, we disengage ourselves from our surroundings and withdraw into ourselves. The desire for an individual existence and for the experience of our corporeality makes itself felt in our growing tired and we sink into it in sleep, surrendering to the powers that restore the body and heal it from the harm brought upon it when awake.

Here we are approaching the mystery of sleep. Though its true nature is at first veiled from us by deep unconsciousness we may yet gain some idea of it from its effects. How inharmonious for example can little children be when they have not slept enough or when they have suddenly been woken up. On the other hand how loving they can be, taking in the world around, when they are filled with the harmonies brought into their waking life from the world of sleep. We have become all too familiar with a certain fact that should fill us with fresh astonishment each day. Every morning we bring from the world of night a living interest for the world, which carries with it the seed of our capacity to love and our joyful dedication to our earthly tasks.

Recognition of this fact can engender a feeling for the sanctity of sleep, and thence a reverence towards that unknown power to whom we must yield our consciousness every night, and from whose hands we may receive it again renewed and harmonized. This can be the starting-point in religious education of children. Indeed it is the beginning of the soul's religious relationship with an unseen world.

The peoples of antiquity looked up in devotion to

1. WAKING AND SLEEPING

that same power which every night takes into itself our consciousness, preserves it intact for us and renders it again in the morning refreshed. They sensed with awe a higher and more comprehensive being, in which the human soul might feel its refuge.

'He who keeps you will not slumber,' the psalmist once sang (121:3). That divine being, worshipped under the name of the LORD in the Old Testament, was felt by the devout in the kingdom of the night. They saw in him that all-comprehending, all-wise being, in whom they were immersed each night, from whom no secret purpose was hidden, in whose rays the soul was judged and also received direction for its thoughts and striving.

The saying (Ps.127:2 author's translation), often smiled at today ' . . . he gives it to his beloved in sleep', expresses a deep experience. People who can still feel something of this cosmic power will readily observe the custom of 'sleeping on' decisions of moment; they will carry a question through one or several nights of sleep before making a decision. The clarifying, mysteriously ordering wisdom which can work into our daytime thinking and deciding from the kingdom of night has been tried out and recognized with astonishment by innumerable people. Such experiences can impel a more and more conscious approach to sleep. The soul will come to the mood of prayer which can bear it rightly over the threshold of sleeping and waking up. The animal slips unconsciously over this threshold. But because the human being can cross it consciously he is ennobled and raised above the level of a creature bound to its urges.

The mood of a true evening prayer will always derive from the trust in that all embracing I AM which is ready to give refuge to our weak self during our sleep.

Morning prayer calls for a mood of gratitude that the soul has been given back from the hidden kingdom of night and feels strengthened for fresh activity. Much is done for the development of a child if he is taught the right practice of evening and morning prayer from early on. A foundation is laid for a harmonious relationship with those worlds which can provide it with healthy forces of the self for its life on earth and also with the capacity for love. Again and again poets have sung of this mystery of the night and of sleep, as Coleridge in the *Rime of the Ancient Mariner* (v):

> Oh sleep! it is a gentle thing,
> Beloved from pole to pole!
> To Mary Queen the praise be given!
> She sent the gentle sleep from Heaven,
> That slid into my soul

Keats, too, expresses the healing power in 'To Sleep':

> O soft embalmer of the still midnight!
> Shutting, with careful fingers and benign,
> Our gloom-pleased eyes, embower'd from the light,
> Enshaded in forgetfulness divine;
> O soothest Sleep! if so it please thee, close,
> In midst of this thine hymn, my willing eyes,
> Or wait the amen, ere thy poppy throws
> Around my bed its lulling charities;
> Then save me, or the passed day will shine
> Upon my pillow, breeding many woes;
> Save me from curious conscience, that still lords
> Its strength for darkness, burrowing like a mole;
> Turn the key deftly in the oiled wards,
> And seal the hushed casket of my soul.

1. WAKING AND SLEEPING

By acknowledging the hidden depths of the kingdom of night, they acknowledge him who was born in the Holy Night, that the day, the world of appearances of the senses, might be healed by the power of love.

2. The rhythm of the week

There are rhythms within the human being which can be detected only when we observe intimately and inwardly. Society was profoundly affected by the introduction of the seven-day week among the peoples of the Middle East some thousands of years ago. About the beginning of the Christian era the seven-day week began to be adopted among the Greeks and Romans and thence with the spread of Christianity it made its mark as an ethical force on the whole of western civilization. In antiquity the seven days of the week were named after the seven planets, and indeed were consecrated to the planetary gods: Saturday to Saturn, Sunday to the Sun, Monday to the Moon, Tuesday to Tyr or Tiwaz, or to Mars (French, *mardi*), Wednesday to Wotan (Odin) or Mercury (French, *mercredi*), Thursday to Thor or Jupiter (*jeudi*) and Friday to Frigg (Freya) or Venus (*vendredi*). Do not these names suggest that men felt subject to the influences of the stars? They turned their gaze to the astral influences which flowed in their life of feeling in the cyclic rhythm of the seven days and which work in the desires and urges that lie below the threshold of waking consciousness. They accord with the laws of the musical scale which ascends in seven notes and reaches the beginning again with the eighth, one octave higher, and thus they resemble a spiral movement winding upwards. It is the hidden dreamer in man who is subject to this rhythm of seven. We can see its laws operating particularly

2. THE WEEK

strikingly in the course of certain illnesses. Think of pneumonia and its fever-curve and how it reaches a crisis on the seventh day. First we observe an ascending movement showing in the inflammatory tendencies and being counteracted by the fever. The sudden drop in temperature which nearly always occurs on the seventh day may mean the abatement of the illness, or else — and then the crisis can be dangerous — only the weakening of that counteraction of which the fever is the expression. Now a similar law, which can only be detected by attentive observation, is constantly in operation in the life of the soul. Fine processes of inflammation are constantly at work in our passions, our sympathies and antipathies. For instance enthusiasm is 'kindled' for an idea or a person or a new task. This tendency has its good and its dangerous side. It can give to our actions true living interest, but also an inclination to 'gush', to blind fanaticism and to passion that robs us of our freedom. For this is the selfish quota that is mixed in our feelings before they have been purified. In it is revealed 'the sickness of sin' in human nature, the result of the Fall, the heritage of Lucifer to mankind, when man's being was torn from the harmony of the divine rhythm of life.

The fundamental impulse of the religion of the Old Testament was to recognize this sickness of mankind and to find the cure for it. Yahweh, the God of the Hebraic revelation, appeared as the bearer of the forces needed by human nature to counteract the working of Lucifer. The Law of Moses presented a comprehensive educational culture designed to permeate a whole people with those moral forces that can suppress all that is selfish. Thus the righteous man of the Old Testament regarded the observance of the law of the sabbath as

13

the crowning of the Mosaic Law. Today we find very curious and strange the scrupulousness and punctiliousness with which the scribes and Pharisees surrounded the sanctity of the sabbath. But we should not forget the great earnestness and faithfulness with which for centuries a people practised this keeping of the seventh day, and so established an extremely powerful rhythm. A tremendous effect is made upon an individual's soul-life and upon the cultural world in that the eagerness of the working day, the work-fever mounting through six days, is always suppressed on the seventh day. All that is lived out in earthly vocation during the week is made to come to total rest on the seventh day. On the seventh day the righteous man is to devote his hours to searching the Law and to seeking to know the divine will, and so to bringing about a complete reversal of the whole direction of his own will. For six days he worked outwardly and exhausted himself to a certain degree. On the seventh day he had to learn to keep still; he had to receive a divine will shining inward from without. In such an institution, created out of a deep insight into the laws of human nature, a social therapy is active, the importance of which cannot be too highly rated.

This wholesome law has been recognized and taken up by Christianity since the beginning, although the first day of the week was put in the place of the seventh as the holy day. This, the Day of the Sun, was assigned to Christ and called the 'Lord's Day' (*Dies Dominica*), for it was upon a Sunday morning that the Lord broke open the grave in which his disciples had laid his crucified body. This power of resurrection that can overcome all heaviness of earth was to be renewed by the Christian as he stood at the beginning of each week. With forces that vanquish death he was to

2. THE WEEK

address himself joyfully to the tasks which the working week laid upon him. The sabbath and its law of rest only aimed at suppressing what had built up too strongly through earthly activity; the Sunday with its keeping alive of the Easter event has the aim of making man's higher spiritual nature so active each week, that when it plunges into its earthly tasks it will not suffer harm but be victorious in its encounters with earth's heaviness. It must be said, however, that the traditional Christian Sunday has been modelled far too closely upon the manner of the sabbath rest. An Easter-Christianity of the future will sanctify Sunday by raising it to a festival of Resurrection. This is the purport of the celebration of the Act of Consecration of Man which is central to a movement of Christian renewal. The Act of Consecration in The Christian Community can be a social healing force in our de-Christianized civilization when it is taken up by a sufficient number of souls in the rhythm of the seven days, and begins to shine strongly into our working lives.

3. The moon rhythm

We become aware of a rhythm which affects the whole human organism even more deeply when we observe the four phases of the moon and their effect upon nature. It is the rhythm of roughly four times seven days. It is most readily revealed in the fluid element. We need only to remember the phenomenon of ebb and flow which we may observe at the sea shore. The phases of the moon have a definite effect upon the weather which can be recorded, especially on the amount of rain, only here of course the weather is dependent also on all sorts of other influences affecting the atmosphere, and therefore the moon's effects cannot always be clearly distinguished.

Since very ancient times the peoples of the world have considered plant growth, the sprouting of the seed, and the blessing of the harvest to be connected with the moon. In ancient times the gods or goddesses of fertility were moon-deities. The times of mating and of parturition in the animal kingdom, and the times of birth in the sequence of human generations came under the moon's mysterious sway. The countryman had ancient rules for sowing and planting according to the phase of the moon. He believed that the seeds sprouted better with the waxing moon while root plants thrived better when planted with the waning moon. The moon indeed sends its influence into the flow of sap in the plant. A new understanding of these laws of growth is presented by careful biological experiments made

3. THE MOON RHYTHM

during the last decades.* These substantiate in every detail how life-processes on earth are subject to the influence of cosmic rhythms.

The human organism is affected also by the rhythm of the four times seven days, and this influence extends to the life of the soul with its moods in so far as it is dependent on the circulation of the fluids. The moon rhythm can be seen most clearly in the female organism. But it can also be detected in the inner life of the male. In both sexes the waxing and waning of the powers of imagination, the periods of spiritual productivity and passivity are subject to the rhythm of the moon's phases. Of course it would be wrong to think that this inner ebb and flow is dependent on the actual phases of the moon. That applies possibly only to the stimulus given to the life of dreams, which for some people reaches a climax with the full moon; and of course to moon-affected sleep-walkers. These phenomena show the last remains of man's former dependence on the cosmos. But the moon rhythm with which we are concerned is completely freed from the influences of the external moon.

In the course of its evolution the human organism has freed itself to a very considerable extent from its foundation in nature. This emancipation is also to be seen in the rhythm of waking and sleeping which although normally corresponding to the rhythm of the earth's rotation upon its axis is not bound to the rising and setting of the sun. Unlike most animals we do not need to go to sleep when the hens roost and rise when the cocks crow, we can adjust the rhythm arbitrarily. Only

* See, for instance, L. Kolisko's *Moon and Plant Growth*, Kolisko Archive; or E. M. Kranich's *Planetary Influences upon Plants*, Bio-Dynamic Literature.

when we neglect or completely abuse it do we destroy the healthy foundation upon which is built our consciousness and its harmonious relationship with its surroundings. It is much the same with the inner moon-rhythm, which in the future people should learn to use in freedom. What we do in the way of education and upbringing, and especially in self-training, works into those hidden formative forces under the sway of the moon, and transforms the inner moon in us. Novalis wrote in one of his fragments: 'We are now educating the moon.' This can only have meaning when applied to the inner cosmos of man, otherwise it remains purely a fantastic notion.

In the mysteries of antiquity and in the symbolism of religion the inner laws of human development were expressed in such pictures. How often have not Christian artists portrayed the apocalyptic vision seen by John on Patmos of the woman with the moon beneath her feet. Crowned with the twelve stars she appears 'clothed with the sun' as the great heavenly sign for our future spiritual life.

What does it represent? The forces of the moon controlled the life of the body and bound the soul naturally to it. Through the powers of the cosmic sun she was victorious over the forces of the moon and able to release herself from nature's bondage. It is the forces of the moon which lead us into incarnation and they work in everything that subjects us to the laws of heredity. Our temperament, our moods, are determined by the way, be it healthy or unhealthy, in which the fluids circulate within our bodies. These fluids were formerly called 'humours'. A person in whom they are in good order is a 'good-humoured' person. The sanguine (*sanguis* is the Latin for blood) temperament

3. THE MOON RHYTHM

kindles easily because its physical constitution can be quickly flooded through with blood. The melancholic owes its viscosity and temporary darkening to the influence of the black bile (or gall) as its name expresses (*melan* is Greek for black, *cholē* is bile). Nothing of the essential nature of the human being is revealed in the temperaments. They only reflect the degree in which the individual has come to terms with his body and its life processes, how deeply he is enmeshed in them or independent of them. The temperaments are primarily something given by nature.

We can best demonstrate how they work by imagining a circle. Our soul must go round this circle, now being immersed in the depths of the physical organism, and now working free again. The circuit is made within the moon rhythm. A soul completely submerged in the body feels burdened with the weight of earth and is 'heavy of heart'. Released again from the internment in the body it soars up with airy light-ness. In such a condition it is inclined to 'levity'. In drawing the circle of the temperaments we should set the melancholic at the bottom and the sanguine at the top. On one side belongs the choleric and on the other the phlegmatic, so that in descending and taking a grip of ourselves in bodily existence we shall incline to a choleric mood — for we begin to feel the resistance of earthly things and come up against it. Again when we begin to feel the release from the bonds of the body we tend to be phlegmatic, for the relaxation is beneficent, but after the severe paralysis we cannot at first find the strength to soar up again. Our soul-life goes round this cycle once in every moon rhythm but the individual's predominant temperament depends upon the way in which his soul manages to come to terms with his body.

There are people, for example, who live so strongly in the memory of what was once 'heavy' (difficult) for them that they do not notice how life has once more carried them aloft; others live so much in the moment that they can quickly shake off all that would cripple them, once it is past, or even because of the mobility of their powers of imagination already feel themselves on the way up when the grip of the body's heaviness has hardly begun to loosen. If we try to feel our way into the nature of the temperaments, we shall come to the conclusion that everyone has within himself the predisposition to all four. We have only to discover them within ourselves in order to find the art of bringing them into inner balance. It cannot be an ideal for us to become completely without temperament for each is really a gift when we understand how to extract its secret blessing. The transformation and harmonization of all four lay the foundation of a true cultivation of the human being. Here we touch upon the secret of all self-training: the victory of the sun-forces over the moon nature in us.

Out of an insight into these laws the great festivals of the year were created. The falling of Easter on the first Sunday after the spring full moon points symbolically to the cosmic mystery of Christianity. In the sign of the mounting strength of the sun Christ achieves the victory over the power of the moon. From this vantage point we can see why certain festivals have a rhythm of four weeks. For example, the Christian calendar appoints four Sundays for Advent. What is to be achieved by the proper cultivation of the Advent mood? It is the healing of the disposition to melancholy

3. THE MOON RHYTHM

induced by the contemplation in November of the transience of all earthly life and by the coming of the early darkness and frost. While the outer world is going to its death and immobility, while the nights grow longer as they draw towards the winter solstice, we should kindle an inner light of hope; we should live towards him who vouchsafes a future to mankind. For the nurture of the soul of the child it can be of the greatest importance to learn to cherish the mood of Advent in the home during the four Advent Sundays. The lighting of the candles as the early evenings fall, the preparation of Christmas presents that will fill the coldness of the world with the warmth of the heart, the expectant counting of the days, all these bring the soul step by step nearer to Christmas, that is to bring relief to all need. By caring for these festival moods from childhood, we may work at the metamorphosis of the temperaments. Advent in particular helps to lighten and to free the melancholic temperament; and because it works into the moon nature of the human being it must be served by a rhythm of four weeks.

A Christianity not merely carrying on the dying traditions, but re-creating the festivals of the year through a clear insight into the spiritual nature of the human being and the world, must attach the greatest importance to such rhythmical ordering. For instance the time of Epiphany, which leads out of the thirteen Holy Nights towards the light of the rising year, will be given the form of a counterpart to Advent. In the ritual life of The Christian Community the time of Epiphany, the festival of Christ's appearing in earthly existence, is also celebrated in a rhythm of four Sundays. This law also applies to the time of the Passion (Lent) as well as to the midsummer festival of St John's Tide, and to the autumn festival at Michaelmas. These two latter festivals are not just celebrated on one appointed day (June 24 and September 29) but within a rhythm of four Sundays they display their whole wealth and spiritual power to those celebrating them.

4. The rhythm of forty in human development

There is another greater rhythm to which the physical nature of our bodies is subject. It comprises the period of four times seven times ten days. It is the ten lunar months or forty weeks which the human embryo normally requires to reach full maturity. This period belongs to the rhythm of the woman's organism which is different from that of the man's. The embryonic development taking place in the womb is controlled by the forty-week rhythm of the female organism.

This period is marked in the Christian calendar in a wonderful way. December 24 bears the name of 'Adam and Eve.' It is to remind the soul, preparing for the festival of the birth of Christ, of the origin of the human race in paradise. We are to be made aware of the significance of the Christmas event: the renewal of the human race through the Second Adam, Jesus Christ. When we receive the Christmas message in the right way we can feel placed again at the beginning of life. The soul is to become Mary. A seed of light can be conceived in her in the Holy Night. It should grow and in the course of the new year take shape. If we take the calendar and reckon the period of forty weeks from Christmas Eve we come exactly to September 29, Michaelmas Day. When we become aware of such ordering we begin to feel great reverence for the wisdom that is to be found in the calendar. For the festival of Michaelmas, presenting our souls with the picture of the dragon-fighter, the powerful contender for the dignity of man, calls upon us to stand firm in earth existence. The tender seed which we were given in the Christmas night should manifest itself in maturity and force of will at Michaelmas.

There is a yet more intimate rhythm that repeatedly appears in religious traditions. It is the period of forty days. It is known that this period, which is one seventh of the period of human embryonic development, is significant at the beginning of the child's life, for the developing human being requires about forty days to so ensoul the body that the latter may give expression to what the soul is feeling. Towards the end of the sixth week the child begins to laugh and so, to the joy of those around him, reveals the magic of his innocent life of feeling.

In earlier times it was felt that the mother should remain withdrawn from external life during this period after the child's birth. According to the Law of Moses she had to undergo the rite of 'purification'. This is mentioned in St Luke's Gospel when Mary and Joseph bring the child Jesus up to Jerusalem in order to make the sacrifice of the doves in the Temple. This takes place 'when the time came for their purification according to the law of Moses' (Luke 2:22), that is forty days after the birth in Bethlehem (The Roman Catholic calendar of festivals calls this day, February 2, the Purification of the Blessed Virgin Mary or Candlemas). This period of forty days comprises the thirteen Holy Nights and the four weeks of Epiphany, the festival dedicated to the mystery of Christ's incarnation.

The Gospels describe how Christ, after the Baptism in Jordan when the heavenly spheres were opened above him and the spirit of worlds descended upon

4. THE RHYTHM OF FORTY

him, withdrew into the desert for a period of forty days and fasted in order to prepare himself for his mission. The spirit has placed him again at the beginning of life. For when we understand that the Baptism in Jordan is really the birth of Christ, that only now did the divine being of Christ enter the body of Jesus of Nazareth, we shall also understand that those forty days of isolation in the desert, culminating in the temptations by the Adversary, are the mighty struggle of the Christ spirit to become truly man. These experiences correspond to what the child goes through during the forty-day period in ensouling the bodily sheath; the difference, however, is that the Christ spirit ensouled the body of Jesus in full waking consciousness in forty days. We know that the mystics of the Middle Ages would lay aside a period of forty days for their ascetic practice before their solitary contemplation. It was felt that just this period was required for the spirit to gain control over the body and to suffuse its gloom with light. Furthermore the same rule was observed in the hygiene of olden times. In the Middle Ages a bar of *quaranta giorni* was placed on ships entering Italian ports when they were suspected of carrying plague, whence we have the word 'quarantine' applied to isolation for the prevention of infection. Out of an ancient medical wisdom the concept has survived that processes of purification in the body — and thereby also the expulsion of the germs of infection — required a forty-day period for their completion.

The Old Testament repeatedly mentions this period. We remember that significant experience of Elijah striving in the wilderness for the salvation and renewal of the revelation of Yahweh. It is told how he was awakened by an angel of the Lord and strengthened with a wonderful food that he might go on a journey of forty days and forty nights to Mount Horeb (1Kings 19:4–8). Here the Bible indicates an inner way of strengthening which the prophet had to tread in order to be able to receive the revelation from Mount Horeb which had formerly been given to Moses. It is equally important that the time of Israel's sojourn in the desert under Moses' leadership is told as being forty years. What applies to the life of a human being in days is numbered in years for a people. The Exodus from Egypt and the giving of the Law on Sinai are manifestations of the impulse towards the evolution of a people. The higher self of the people of Israel entered the earthly sheath of this nation with these events. It was the birth of a mighty folk-soul which took place under Moses' spiritual leadership; and the forty years of desert education, which the people had to undergo before they might enter the promised land, correspond to that intimate time-rhythm which the child has to pass in seclusion at the beginning of earthly life.

Once again the same period appears in the ordering of the Christian festivals as the rhythm that leads from Easter to Ascension. It is that period of grace granted to the disciples to be in the company of the Risen One. These forty days also signify a beginning of life; for the Death on Golgotha is a birth of the spirit. In the events which take place between Good Friday and the Easter morn, the Christ-spirit battles through to its new form of existence. Henceforth it is to be the spirit of the earth. It begins to permeate the life of this dying planet with its rejuvenating divine forces. In those forty days when the figure of the Risen One shone before the disciples' eyes the Christ began to enter into the earth's atmosphere and fill it with his soul and power before being taken up into the clouds. Since then he is united

4. THE RHYTHM OF FORTY

with the whole life of the earth. Every year when springtime awakes, the human soul should open anew to the living wonder of our earth. But we should not feel the earth without the spirit of love, the Christ, that reigns in it. Therefore in this festive rhythm of forty days from Easter to Ascension it is important that we learn to experience ever and anew the birth of the spirit of Christ in the life of the earth.

5. Sun Rhythms

It is moon rhythms that bring us into earthly life. We
lived in them before we entered through the gate of
birth into the sheath of our earthly body. They work
on in us as a cosmic heritage determining what we are.
But it is sun rhythms that call us to full awakening in
earth existence. They free our self from the bonds of
the past and give it courage to live towards the future.
As we become more and more conscious of all that is
taking place between sun and earth in the course of the
year we can at the same time receive the ideals to lift
us beyond ourselves and the strength to realize them in
earthly life.

The sun rhythm of the year is most apparent in the
plant world. If the human soul were to go no further
than the contemplation of this sprouting, blossoming,
ripening and withering nature it would feel enclosed
within a circuit of unalterable processes with its own life
exposed to the transient. A complementary view is
needed from quite a different direction. Let us consider
how the corn in the fields and the fruit trees produce
more seed than is necessary for their reproduction. This
superabundance of life-force is sacrificed to form the
grain and fruit which serves as nourishment for more
highly developed organisms. Thus every year the plant
world prepares the sustenance for the life of the animal
and human kingdoms. It is untrue (or at least a one-
sided theory) that nature knows only the struggle for
existence and only nurtures the urge to maintain the

individual and the species. Nature's readiness to sacrifice is manifest in all growth and fruition that impels her creatures to give of their life and to provide beyond their own needs that they may serve higher stages of life. The human being owes his ability to live upon this planet to this all-pervading sacrificial will in Nature.

In the rhythm of the sun's activity with its light that wakens life, with its warmth that brings ripening, the earth is bathed in those exalted forces in which we must recognize a cosmic morality. When the human being recognizes these laws of the life of the sun he can consciously absorb them. They can be reborn in his heart as the creative life of love. They will inspire him to deeds of love which can raise human life above its selfish circle of existence. For why should not the human being with his maturing soul and spirit powers also serve as food for higher realms of existence instead of dissipating himself entirely in the urge of self-assertion and in the preservation of the species? Should he not also, like the plants for animal and man, become nourishment for higher worlds?

Let us consider certain species of animals and how they are constrained by the year's vegetative rhythm. The stag casts his antlers every year, and not only does he renew them, but every year adds two more points, so that in fact his age can be read from the number of the points of his antlers. Or note the moulting of birds in the autumn. Every year they renew their feathers. The human being is not required to perform such a remarkable feat, and so he does not have to expend the productive forces needed for it annually. And here we come to a justified question: what does he do with these unexpended forces? Keeping to the picture, we may say that from the forces of his soul he can produce a spiritual coat of feathers to fly with. As winter approaches and he begins to turn inwards he can feel called upon to let thoughts spring up from within; he can activate the creative power of imagination which will give him an inner *élan* and inner warmth when nature with her gifts from without has left him to himself. But this weaving of forces in the inner man differs in one point from the creativity which renews the birds' feathers in autumn. The human being can let his creative forces lie fallow. The powers of nature look after the birds, but the human being is called to freedom.

The ancient peoples, who felt they were embedded in the rhythm of the seasons, created the great festivals out of such insights. So we find that everywhere where the ancient mystery-wisdom predominated, the autumn festivals were specially marked. When the outer world with its life-giving abundance withdraws from the human being, then it is for him to become active from within, to become aware of the creative forces slumbering in his being's depths and to bring them to development. Festivals such as the Eleusinian celebrated in Greece or the cult of Adonis in Asia Minor were designed to rouse man to himself. They were designed to teach him to grasp himself in his creative freedom and so awaken the immortal being within him. If in our time the Michael festival is celebrated, not from an old calendar tradition, but from a new spiritual knowledge that can consciously apprehend the Michaelic forces streaming towards mankind, it will enable the soul to awaken the eternal within in the meeting of autumn, and to find the indestructible in the face of the destruction, doom and transcience of the world.

5. SUN RHYTHMS

Today the human being is freeing himself more and more from the natural basis of his life. Unless he can form again consciously a relationship with the rhythm of the revolving year, this development will lead finally to a complete inner poverty of soul, with a weakening of personality and the atrophy of his capacity for experience.

There is a being who will come to his aid in this conscious experiencing of the year. Just as the external sun is a necessity of life for nature and its revelations, so is the Christ for the human soul and its development towards the spirit. In earlier ages, it was from the widths of the universe that the Christ-being was borne into earth-existence with the sun-rhythm of the year. The seers of old perceived him in the reigning of the sun and when they revered the God of Light (by whatever name they called him) they were speaking of him. Since through his sacrificial death he united himself lovingly with the life of our planet, he has breathed his holy sun forces into its existence.

He will lead this earth and humanity to an exalted transformation when men are filled with his presence in the breathing rhythm of the year; when human beings learn to feel how, in winter, he goes down into the depths of matter and in those depths is ever born anew as a sun-seed; when they let themselves be borne aloft in summer towards the light with which, arising from the earthly tomb, he is wedded again year by year. Such a view of Christ which regards and reveres him as a cosmic being is quite foreign to our time; it sees the value of his redemptive deed not just in the salvation of the human soul but in its cosmic import. It will become understandable again only when we regard the earth itself as a living being. What is opposed to such a conception is not the Bible, as is often thought, for on all its pages the Bible bears witness to it, but the materialistic outlook of the last centuries. Today, however, we see a reversal in the scientific view of earth which was formed out of one-sided mathematical-physical methods over the last centuries. These could present the universe only as a soul-less conglomerate of matter, sometimes of glowing gas, sometimes reduced to ash and dust. The coming age has the task of winning back an organic world picture. Geology and meteorology are being forced by the language of the facts to recognize that the earth in its layers and especially in the atmosphere is a wonderfully integrated living oranism whose rhythms may be perceived.*

From this recognition it is but a step to accepting what poets of all the ages have sensed and proclaimed, and what the ancient religions cherished in their creeds and worship: namely that our earth has a soul. And Christ has become the higher self of the soul of the earth. That was what enabled him to say at the Last Supper, when in a sacrifice of love he began to unite with the life of the earth: 'This is my body, this is my blood.' The holy Last Supper is more than a symbol of the presence of Christ in earth existence. Within a sheath of the earthly nourishment of bread and wine, a divine being is giving himself to the life of the dying earth in order to lead it to its transfiguration.

Now we can understand in what direction we need an added perspective when we experience the seasons of the year. The Christian festivals serve to awaken perception of the presence of the Christ in the rhythms

---

* See, for instance, Guenther Wachsmuth's *Erde und Mensch*, Philosophisch-Anthroposophisch; or James Lovelock's *Gaia: A New Look at Life on Earth*, Oxford University Press.

of nature. Let us then take these festivals in the order of the four turning points of the year as they occur in the temperate zone of the Northern hemisphere where the seasons are most clearly defined. It was in these lands that Christianity could extend most strongly in history and culture, and it was among the peoples of this zone that the Christian festivals with their rich symbolism and inwardness of soul were developed.

When the earth's soul in the great breathing rhythm of the year turns completely inward, the life of the earth shuts itself off from the cosmos. The ground crystallizes in the winter cold; the sap withdraws; the plant world retracts its life-forces into the tiny seed. At this time we too must begin to live inwardly, learning to see the shining being of the earth in the darkness of earthly substance, to see the Christ-Spirit that is awake in the heart of the earth while outer nature falls asleep. If we look at this time only to the picture of the vanishing vegetation, of nature that has died away, then the death-forces of the earth will seize us. A heaviness comes upon the soul, closing from its awareness the mysterious depths of the earth where a higher sunlike life is born.

The circle of the temperaments which reflect the soul's interplay with our bodily nature finds its counterpart in the circle of the four moods of the year as experienced by the earth-soul. More exactly we may say: it is the innumerable swarms of nature-spirits which in the life of the earth are now under a deep spell and again rise rejoicing from their imprisonment. When for example we observe the melancholy which often comes irresistibly over the soul in the mists of November, we cannot always find the cause of it in the experience of personal destiny. It is the unredeemed waiting with 'eager longing' of the creation of which St Paul speaks, the 'groaning in travail' of the elemental beings (Rom 8:19,22). The soul of the human being is overcome by it when he does not know that they are waiting for him as for their redeemer who is to lead them up again to the light.

In experiencing the breathing of the earth in the course of the year we pass through the four elements: through earth in the winter frost and darkness of matter, through wateriness in the coming alive of the forces of spring, through the light-filled air of the months of blossom around the summer solstice, and through consuming fire in the harvest time of the year. This passage has its counterpart in the passage of the soul through the temperaments. We have already discussed the Christmas festival with its preparation through the four Advent Sundays and its aftermath in the four weeks of Epiphany. This festival time bears within it those healing forces necessary to free the melancholic in us, for it opens our vision to the future of the earth, it snatches melancholy away on wings of hope from the paralysing power that binds the soul to the past and what is becoming fixed and set.

The melancholic person is greatly concerned with his personal affairs. He can feel only his own pain. And so Christmas, the Festival of Love, calling upon us to think of others' need and to give joy to other hearts, is the true counterbalance for this temperament. For once the melancholic has been led out above himself: he best of all can feel intimately the sufferings and straits in the destinies of his fellow men.

The watery forces that in early spring loosen the ground and cause vegetation to sprout threaten to wrap the life of feeling in insensitivity. Then the soul that surrenders passively to the vegetative forces of the body becomes phlegmatic. Out of such an insight medieval Christianity prescribed strict fasting for the early spring (and indeed for a period of forty days). Fasts were to prepare a mood for the Passion. The phlegmatic is he who needs a sound shaking to wake him out of his life's dullness. The Cross of Golgotha is set in the early spring, reminding us that a divine being took upon himself the guilt and suffering of earthly man. Strength to bear the sorrows of others is the strength of the phlegmatic temperament once it has been shaken up and can see that a certain task is to be accomplished.

The air filled with sunshine bringing forth the blossom of May-time lifts the soul above all the weight of earth. The easily-inflammable temperament, the sanguine in us, is wakened by this happy time of year. The flower, lifting its calyx to the sun, the moth fluttering round the flower, the fireflies swarming in the summer night, in them all is revealed the earth-soul, borne away at this time into the etheric worlds. And the human soul opening to such beauty, should it not also be borne on high? The positive strength of the sanguine temperament lies in its capacity for enthusiasm which it can place at the disposal of some great idea. It is always ready to start off on something new, but instead of losing itself in its own enjoyment it has to learn to serve with faithfulness. Beside his innate vitality the sanguine person must develop the ability to renounce. The Festival of John the Baptist sets in the high station of the sun the archetypal saint who by his powers of enthusiasm could have moved a world grown old, but who in renunciation stepped back behind the greater one to come. When the Festival of St John is rightly celebrated it will engender in the soul the will to become still and, following the example of nature's summer life of fruition, let ripen the wisdom of old age which can never be attained without renunciation.

In the outbursts of the thunderstorms in midsummer, in the ripening and sweetening of the fruits, in the bursting into flame of the autumn colours in the woods and gardens is revealed the fire-nature which at harvest time glows through and illuminates all earth life, but which finally would consume all. This fire-nature, when it fills the human being, becomes lust for action; often it seeks outlet in an explosive temperament. It is as if the creative spiritual forces of the earth would sink deeper into substance as autumn comes on in order to drive the nourishing fruits to a final maturity in a wonderful alchemy of essences. Force held in check works its autumnal miracle in the ripening of the earth, but it can also erupt suddenly from the clouds in thunder and lightning.

On August nights the heavens send down shining swarms of shooting stars and so spray the earth's atmosphere with meteoric dust. It is as if a cosmic physician would apply a strong iron-therapy to the feverish inflamed organism of the earth like Michael conquering the dragon with his sword. Our age is full of fiery forces dammed back and pressing for outlet. They are constantly threatening to explode destructively in society as long as they are not understood and illuminated. The choleric becomes a revolutionary unless he is allowed to apply his powers meaningfully. But he can also become a fighter for social justice and human freedom when the ideals of earthly existence begin to dawn upon him. The cure of the choleric nature lies in being given a definite and worthwhile task in order to develop his energies through coming up against oppo-

5. SUN RHYTHMS

sition. The choleric person suffers from the need to make himself felt: he has to become aware of his own personal worth. This he can do best through achievements which require him to master situations or himself. He needs a great and noble aim. The mighty picture of Michael's struggle against the dragon's power contains the inspiring forces which can release the proper initiatives of the soul. Present-day humanity requires such an archetypal picture; otherwise it will be driven into the abyss of self-destruction. An apocalyptic vision of our times and an apocalyptic responsibility towards our times must set the tone which will make the festival of Michael a strong cultural therapy in our day. It must bring about the miraculous cure of the demonized life of will.

There is a wealth of traditional Christian festivals that belong to wintertime and spring; but the festivals of St John and Michaelmas belong to the half of the year that in the Christian calendar is less celebrated. Today these two festivals are seeds which will grow in content the more nature can shine with spirit forces during St John's tide; and the more we can recognize man's spiritual dignity during Michaelmas. Unless these two festivals can be given a significance equal to the festivals in the other half of the year, the soul will be unable to attain the complementary vision necessary to overcome the sickness of our times: materialism.

The festival times in the rhythm of the year's course open the spiritual gates through which the Christ-being can make his entry into the life of the earth. They hold the powers which can transform all that causes the human being to fall sick in his destiny upon the earth either by condensing and hardening him in the darkness of substance or by dissipating and dissolving him in the lightness of air. The festivals restore the balance for him between the heights and the depths; and by transforming man they work at the transformation of the earth. In this mystery the elemental beings imprisoned in matter will be released when the Christian festivals are rightly celebrated from a knowledge of the rhythmical secrets of the cosmos. The dreaming soul of the earth awakens in the light of Christ and is transfigured in him.

6. The cosmic rhythms of the Platonic Year

When we experience the polarities in summer and winter, spring and autumn, our life of feeling can reach out into the cosmos. Moral impulses are engendered in the soul. Feelings become more selfless and onesidedness is corrected. The polarity of perception and thinking, the summer and the winter moods are appealed to equally by the festivals in the course of the year. So we learn to live in the salubrious swing of the pendulum from the inward strengthening to the outward giving of oneself to the world. Of course this seasonal polarity in the life of the soul is not as sharply defined as we have outlined it, for we are beings gifted with memory; and by memory we carry the experienced mood and what we have gained in inner force from one season to another. In this we have our freedom, for we have grown out of our cosmic ties and can move freely in what has been won in the way of cosmic experience.

It is given to us every year to partake of the great breathing in the life-rhythm of the earth-soul. The earth-being holds in her breath during the winter nights, when our souls can go deeply into the mystery of Christ and the earth, in this time of the thirteen Holy Nights. The earth's spirit is now completely immersed in the earth's substance, and so the earth awakes to herself with the Christ being awake within her. These nights were once considered a separate time of year. Certain Oriental peoples including the ancient Hebrews, made the lunar year the basis of their calendar, and thus had a year of twelve moons, that is 354 days (354 days 9 hours to be more exact). The solar year exceeds this by almost exactly 11 days (10 days 21 hours). Cosmic rhythms never quite fit into each other exactly. Starting with the day of the Epiphany (January 6) and adding the lunar year we come to Christmas, for on December 25 the moon is at nearly the same phase as it was on the January 6 of the same year after having waxed and waned twelve times. Then follow those days by which the sun-rhythm exceeds the twelve moon cycles. A deep cosmic feeling made of this period between the Holy Night and the Epiphany a hallowed time when the human soul was lifted out of the moon's power and could live in dedication to the communion of the sun-spirit with the earth-soul. In this time of the deep winter nights the soul could be graced with the highest inspiration.

A profound memorial to the thirteen Holy Nights has been bequeathed to us by the Nordic seers in the *Dream-Song of Olav Åsteson*. Olav Åsteson fell into a deep sleep on Christmas Eve and wandered with a clairvoyant consciousness through the realms of the dead until he met the Christ. Then he returned to earth-consciousness on the morning of Epiphany and was able to bring to his fellow human beings the great tidings of the higher spiritual worlds.

When we look at the course of the year in this way we see it as the revelation of the life of an all-holy being. We see it as the drawing of one breath by the spirit of Christ uniting with the earth. Within what great cosmic rhythm can this breathing be found? All that goes on between sun and earth in the course of the year is to be found in the writing of the stars as the

6. THE PLATONIC YEAR

sun moves through the twelve constellations of the zodiac. From the geocentric aspect the vernal equinox moves imperceptibly against the background of the stars, and after seventy-two years it falls back one degree in the sky (1° of longitude on the ecliptic); and after about 2160 years it has moved back one whole constellation (30°). After twelve times this period, that is after about 25 920 years, this precession movement has returned to its starting point. Ancient astronomers knew this period well and called it the 'Platonic Year'.

Regarding the Platonic Year as a macrocosmic year we find that the subdivisions of that year also correspond harmoniously with those of a human life. By dividing the cosmic year into 365 cosmic days, each of these cosmic days is about seventy-one years. A human life-span from birth to death corresponds to one macrocosmic day. This life span is 25 920 days.

From the insight into these wonderful correspondences between macrocosmic and microcosmic rhythms we can begin to understand what goes on in the life of nations as the star-year progresses. The great culture-bearing peoples of antiquity revered the constellation in which the vernal point lay in their time. During the Egyptian culture the spring equinox was in the constellation of the Bull. The worship of the Bull or the Cow reflected the consciousness of that cosmic hour.

The worship of the 'golden calf' into which the people of Israel fell back during their wandering in the desert is likewise a recognition of the cosmic forces which were given to the earth from that constellation. But the people of Israel were to pave the way to a new age. Their mission belonged to those forces that came from the Ram. As the sun gradually moved its vernal point from the Bull to the Ram quite new spiritual forces began to shine into the life of our planet. They transformed man's consciousness correspondingly and released new cultural impulses. The sacrifice of the ram which Abraham performed on Mount Moriah was already a forecast of that future epoch towards which his descendants were slowly to ripen. The sacrificing of the Paschal lamb, which according to the Old Testament rite had to be made in the night of the spring full moon, shows the deep connection which the cultural task of the Chosen People had with the forces of the spring sun shining from the constellation of the Ram and reflected in the full moon. Christ as the 'Lamb of God' is again the most exalted expression of these cosmic forces given to man.

With the first Christian spiritual movement however new powers begin to play into the development of human consciousness. The Fish was the original Christian symbol by which in a world grown old, the followers of Christ made themselves known to each other and in which they felt united. They prepared the seed of that cultural impulse which could only come into its own at the beginning of modern times. Young spiritual forces have to grow in the mothering shelter of older and more mature cultural forms. Only when the medieval cultural world began to decay could the Christian spiritual impulse free itself from Latin culture and the Latin way of thinking and also from the Old Testament forms of religion and morality. It will only be able to show itself in its true form, undistorted by outward tradition, when the sun-forces shining from the constellation of the Fishes have won complete victory in human culture.

7. The Saturn rhythm

For a more profound understanding of human destiny it would be necessary to go into the organization of the seven-year rhythms. There we should see how the forces of the planetary world take effect in sequence from childhood right into advanced old age. The eternal individual has his home in the circling of the stars. He can bring to earth existence what he has received as heavenly endowment only in stages, in a rhythm of recurring seven-year periods. But as these seven-year periods are not entirely unfamiliar or unrecognized, we shall now select a less evident planetary rhythm of decisive significance in our lives. This is the Saturn period.

A complete circuit of Saturn through the constellation takes nearly thirty years. The first thirty years of our lives from birth is the period of our formative years. Up to the thirtieth year we are still drawing on those forces of growth which we brought with us into earthly life. They give the soul a natural vitality. It is easy to observe how towards the thirtieth year impulses receive a first check. When a person becomes one Saturn-'year' old the hardening forces appear within the organism.

The god Saturn (the Greeks called him *Kronos*) was always depicted as an old man, often with a scythe. Within the older order of the planets, which did not include Uranus, Neptune and Pluto, he is the guardian of the frontiers of our solar system. His work is to enclose, to draw the limits to the vital impulses given to us as cosmic grace upon our earthly way. And so we may observe — either by self-examination or by looking closely at other destinies — how around the thirtieth year a crisis comes about which shows up either in health disorders or more frequently in crises in the development of the soul. Enthusiasm may be lost, the goals of life look empty, or there can be a clear break in the melody of destiny. People who feel none of this, who, as we might say, 'haven't changed a bit', from now on usually sink into comfortable mediocrity. That does not prevent them from still 'feeling young', because they warm up the experiences of their youth or seek their happiness in repetition, because they have not tried to develop their powers of transformation.

In the older chemistry and medicine certain metals were ascribed to the seven planets, and this was the basis of a metal therapy. According to this ancient knowledge, lead belonged to Saturn. We can imagine that a subtle lead influence is constantly playing upon our life-organization in that we are subject to the influence of the planet Saturn. In the course of a Saturn-year this influence creates within us a hidden lead-man, a kind of shadowy figure which exudes certain hardening tendencies into our whole attitude. In medicine a chronic lead-poisoning — it was known for example that printers suffered from this as an occupational disease — was called 'saturnism'. An accelerated decline of strength — palsy, loss of hair, failing eyesight and so on, is connected with this malady. We can also characterize as 'saturnism' that lead influence imparted to our whole organism in the course of a Saturn-year, even though its effects are much more inward.

7. THE SATURN RHYTHM

When we understand this secret of a rhythm determined by the cosmos, we shall raise the pertinent question concerning the rejuvenating forces for human life. Who gives mankind a second youth?

Now we have a basis for regarding the appearance of Christ in earth existence as a cosmic fact. St Luke's Gospel clearly indicates that Jesus of Nazareth was about thirty years old when he began his ministry. In older writings the words which resound from the heights of heaven at the Baptism are: 'Thou art my beloved son, today I have begotten thee' (Luke 3:22). It is a real new beginning of life, a life from the abundance of cosmic grace which now develops through the three years in the body of Jesus of Nazareth. It brings completely new forces of childhood into ageing mankind.

Towards the end of those three years the unique transformation which had taken place in this body was revealed to the souls of the three disciples who were on the mountain with Christ. The Gospels describe the Transfiguration of Jesus of Nazareth in the words: 'his face shone like the sun, and his garments became white as light' (Matt.17:2). That is the victory of the sun-forces over the Saturn-powers, which had taken place in the life of Christ between the thirtieth and the thirty-third year.

This victory came to its highest revelation only when Christ went his way from the Mount of the Transfiguration to the Hill of Golgotha. On Golgotha Saturn's powers of death were broken by the Sun-Spirit for all time on earth. Thenceforth from Golgotha there shines a power into human hearts, working its everlasting rejuvenating miracle upon man's being that is fallen prey to death. When we unite inwardly with the life of Christ, with his Death and Resurrection we can obtain a second youth; one bestowed by the spirit and manifesting when our natural youth has been consumed by the Saturn rhythm; for Christ, in the middle of his life, went through death that the human soul might live the second half of earthly life from his forces of youth.

When we see how very many people starting life with promising talents begin to lose momentum about thirty, we can understand what a mighty difference it makes for the destiny of the individual if he has been allowed in his young years to unite his heart with the Christ. Now we can measure the gravity of our responsibility for the religious upbringing of the child and the adolescent. We can best lay the foundation for the second half of his life by helping him at the right time and in the right way to feel the touch of the Christ in his heart. Such a soul will then pass differently through that critical time of life which in one way or another will manifest round the thirtieth year. Furthermore we may add, that for a person who is destined to die before reaching that age this inner connection to Christ will show itself victorious in the hour of death. Working in the death forces Saturn's influence normally culminates about the thirtieth year, but in the case of death and sickness that influence is accelerated. The Christ however is always at work, transfiguring the death forces into a higher life, and can give the soul a heavenly youth beyond death's threshold.

When the gift of Christ's love has been received, the cosmic rays of life can work in the heart, renewing the blood. From the early Middle Ages, a spiritual stream knew and reverently cultivated this cosmic aspect of the Christ's sacrifice, which had been lost by then to the traditions of the Church. The legend of the Holy Grail

7. THE SATURN RHYTHM

tells pictorially of these facts. We find in Wolfram von Eschenbach's *Parzival* several indications that when Saturn is at its highest Amfortas's sickness is at its worst and the healing coming from the Grail then begins to be active. Our nature if exposed defencelessly to Saturn's influence becomes ill or suffers some paralysing of its soul-forces. But when that influence is met and transformed by Christ, Saturn becomes a benefactor of human nature, introducing development which can lead to the most supreme spiritualization of the natural forces.

The rhythm of the Saturn-year, and the three Sun-years added by the grace of Christ which transform the death processes into a higher life, make up a period of thirty-three years. This rhythm can appear to us hallowed in the deepest sense by the life of Jesus Christ upon earth. A thirty-three year cycle can be seen in the destiny of significant people and in the cultural impulses of mankind. By tracing it we can come to enlightened insights into the working of the powers of destiny in human life, and we have then a most valuable key to the mysteries of human biography.

The Seven Planets

Adam Bittleston

Today's knowledge of the planets rests on scientific observation. Adam Bittleston takes the astronomical phenomena as his starting point, going on to embrace the intuitions of astronomers, poets and artists from varied cultures.

Billeston brings diverse witnesses: the echoes of the Upanishads and the *Bhagavadgita*, the words of Buddha and Aristotle, the biblical sense for meaning in number, and insights of such minds as those of Kepler, Shelley and Goethe. He weaves these pieces together to give a picture of the planets showing something of their 'soul' and 'spirit'.

The various chapters gradually develop descriptions of the planets. The Moon, easiest to observe, progresses regularly around the zodiac in a miniature correspondence to the Sun. Describing lunar influence in the biosphere, Bittleston them approaches Rudolf Steiner's spiritual investigation, Anthroposophy. This allows consideration of a human existence before birth and after death, linked with the spheres of the planets.

Floris Books